To Brian

with best wishes

Anna

Dear Dylan

An anthology of letters to, and poems after,
Dylan Thomas

Indigo Dreams Publishing

First Edition: Dear Dylan
First published in Great Britain in 2021 by:
Indigo Dreams Publishing Ltd
24 Forest Houses
Halwill
Beaworthy
Devon
EX21 5UU

www.indigodreams.co.uk

Copyright for this anthology © Indigo Dreams Publishing Ltd 2021
Cover image: Andrew Slocombe
Cover design: Ronnie Goodyer, Indigo Dreams
Photographs: Matthew Hughes

ISBN 978-1-912876-57-0
British Library Cataloguing in Publication Data. A CIP record for this book can be obtained from the British Library.

Designed and typeset in Palatino Linotype by Indigo Dreams.

Printed and bound in Great Britain by 4edge Ltd
Papers used by Indigo Dreams are recyclable products made from wood grown in sustainable forests following the guidance of the Forest Stewardship Council.

Andrew Slocombe is an artist and musician, living and working in Bristol. He finds inspiration from a variety of sources, including inside his own head. Andrew's work can be viewed at: andrewslocombe.co.uk

Matthew Hughes is a photographer and creative designer from Laugharne, west Wales. Among other projects, he played a key role as curator of the poet's Swansea birthplace during the Dylan Thomas centenary celebrations in 2014 – extensively researching, and recreating what the poet's bedroom would have resembled at the time that his first book '18 Poems' was published in 1934.

The Boathouse, dusk

About the Editors

Anna Saunders is the author of *Communion* (Wild Conversations Press), *Struck* (Pindrop Press), *Kissing the She Bear* (Wild Conversations Press), *Burne Jones and the Fox, Ghosting for Beginners* and *Feverfew* (all Indigo Dreams Publishing). She has had poems published in numerous journals and anthologies. Anna holds a Masters in Creative and Critical Writing from The University of Gloucestershire and is the CEO and founder of Cheltenham Poetry Festival.

Ronnie Goodyer runs award-winning Indigo Dreams Publishing with partner Dawn. They were the first joint winners of the *Ted Slade Award for Services to Poetry*. Ronnie has seven published collections and was on the BBC2 Judging Panel for their *Off By Heart* poetry competition. He is Poet-in-Residence for the League Against Cruel Sports, and in 2019 edited/published the first poetry anthology in their 100 year history.

A few words from Hannah

The last few months and years of my grandfather's life were difficult as he was both physically and mentally ill, and this is the period most people are familiar with. We should acknowledge the tough times and explore them fully to truly understand Dylan Thomas, however we should also remember my grandfather's achievements during his whole life. By doing this, we will be able to appreciate that he was a talented, hard working and creative individual.

Much of his work is full of the sort of characters we all know, which makes it accessible to a wide audience and has allowed it to become popular in many countries around the world and with many people from different walks of life. His early poetry, though not as easy to understand, is equally fascinating as you observe a teenage boy, furiously experimenting with new ideas and discovering the power of words. You also see a meticulous craftsman.

The poems and letters in 'Dear Dylan' illustrate how he has influenced and affected the lives of the poets featured, their attitudes towards him, at different stages of their lives. I'm delighted with this book – and International Dylan Thomas Day is the perfect date for publication!

Hannah Ellis

A few words from the Editors...

Anna

'Dear Dylan' was inspired by a passion for Dylan's work, a love and admiration also felt by fellow editor, poet and publisher Ronnie Goodyer. We wanted to sing of Dylan in an anthology of letters to, and poems after, this most mellifluous of poets. We were deluged by poems when we put the call out – and it was hard to make a selection with so many strong pieces to choose from.

'Dear Dylan' celebrates Dylan's legacy, and demonstrates how his work continues to inspire writers and artists the world over, years after his death. We hope you will enjoy our final selection – a tribute to the extraordinary talents of a writer who, whether he was writing letters, short stories, scripts or poetry, captured our hearts as he *'set fire to the stars'*.

Ronnie

Back in 2019, partner Dawn (Bauling) and I met Anna in a Cheltenham teashop. The night before we'd had our Indigo Dreams Showcase at the Poetry Festival and were now discussing Anna's personal publishing plans. She read new poems, we commented and all made notes. This became her latest collection, 'Feverfew'. Then we talked about an idea for a Dylan Thomas tribute, an anthology to include Dylan-inspired poems and letters – what our modern poets would like to say to Dylan if he were with us now. It was intriguing, exciting, and we loved it. The idea morphed into 'Dear Dylan' and, after a false 2020 start due to the pandemic, we're delighted to finally publish. We hope you feel the same way about this as we do.

The Writing Shed, Laugharne

CONTENTS

Dear Dylan

Dinner in Fort William – Francesca Albini

Doll head broken neck
Look down. The clouds
Slide down the flanks, your flanks mountain
In a flavour of wrong.
Old man who never young
Stands still out of principle
Eating from a bowl of steam.
Dark clouds me raining from right
To left
To the trees
Away. Garden looks like grave
Sloping mountains of mud.
Mud in a bowl
So stretched out
Is Scotland's time
Irrelevant motionless whispering.
I touch your darkness
In the empty night
And find it warm.

Inspired by Dylan's rhythm and atmosphere

Dear Dylan,

Thank you for accepting to read my poem, and I'm looking forward to your comments. I hope you won't find too much unintended 'creakiness of conflict' in it, although conflict was part of the scenario. I wrote this poem from a rented apartment at the foot of a mountain on a stormy day, thinking of a scattered rhythm inspired by your work. Current scenario: my flat in London, first cold day after a scorching summer, third day back from Scotland, now wading through chaos, letters, bills, suitcases, laundry, fabric, crochet, books, ideas.

I remember when I was young, and you were old. Now I'm older than you will ever be. And I think back to the days spent reading your poems and dreaming of following in your steps. Drinking, searching, touching the first ulcers of life. I wanted wrinkles on my porcelain skin, and that coarse wisdom I thought you had.

Yesterday: at the London Library, reading your letters to Vernon, looking in vain for *Mana*, and ending up reading a book about banana plantations. In my now older wisdom, I find everything linked in a fatal cobweb, you, dram, rain, summer and winter skies.

With gratitude,
Francesca

After Sunday – Audrey Ardern-Jones

The picnickers have gone, children's moats
and pebbled forts are washed away. I climb
down a landing jetty onto a red sandy beach
where Caldey's rocks burst black-grey

over white hems of wash, where waters swirl
in circles. I curl my toes under the rush
of incoming waves and feel the wind slapping
salt air on my face against the rhyme of the tide.

I watch gulls flying inland, they know this place,
their wings angled upright, tight like sails.
They yell and swing sideways as they land
nearby on the shore hoping I'll feed them.

Bells ring from the monastery nearby, monks sing
evening Gregorian chants. The light dips, tufts
of clouds float in sunlight; I see a white gold belt
on the horizon, bright beyond the cliffs.

And this is it, the day is done, the process
in the weather melts the white-gold belt into navy,
light fading, drifting away into darkness. I'm bereft,
I hear ghosts treading sea waters, waiting, waiting...

Inspired by poem: *'A Process In the Weather of the Heart'*

Dear Dylan,

Thank you for your gravy brown voice, your curly hair, deep set eyes and soft round mouth. You've been my poster boy for years – your picture on my wall. I listen to your poems, your plays - I melt at the sound of your Welsh accent, it sends a tickle down my spine. I'd save up my holiday money to come and hear you read - queue for days to buy a ticket. I know you like a drink & I'm up for that! I'd buy you a pint or a whiskey...or perhaps a pint of whiskey!

You might like to know that I've been a reader of your work since I was a raging teenager. I've learned lines of your famous poems...they sing in my head, I sleep talk your language. As well, I love your letters, your many, many letters - in particular the ones you wrote to Caitlin when you were in the States. Your passion thrills me, excites me and lights up the world.

Thank you Dylan, you've fed my spirit in ways of meaning, love and beauty. You live on like the Welsh dragon; you're an icon, a Celtic inspiration.

Yours,
Audrey

Seasoned – Nick Browne

We can talk of boyhood, lust and potency,
lambent nature wild in its winnowing wrecking,
in its force and splintering rage.

A tumult of tension, the racking tautening
pulling apart in crack of wishbone, all men,
heroic in their anguished loss.

Our past is different, though no less fierce.
We, tempered by forge fires, roiling inner storms,
ride like gulls on the turn-slide of the wave.

We are furies, sirens, dryads, crones,
one with the othered, old adversaries,
seasoned, not torn by time, surfing the tide.

Dear Dylan,

I struck one day by luck you, my friend there, with the winning air. The force that drives the water through the rocks drives my red blood. Your heart is luminous.

I hug to love with my unruly scrawl. I learnt man's tongue, to twist the shapes of thoughts into the stony idiom of the brain, to shoot and sing your praise.

What is the metre of the dictionary? I never thought to utter or think. I have been told to reason by the heart, but heart, like head, leads helplessly. I have longed to move away and dug your grave in my breast, the jealous coursing of the unrivalled blood. Hold you poison or grapes? Do you not father me, made me happy in the sun?

The child shall question all his days. I bitterly take to task my poverty and my craft. The grave and my calm body are shut to your coming as stone. Lie in grace.

To take to give is all, return what is hungrily given, the lovely gift of the gab. In my craft and sullen art, O may my hearts' truth still be sung.

 Fancy a pint?
Nick

(All but the last taken from Dylan Thomas: Collected Poems (original edition) New Directions Publishing 2010)

Prophet – Michael Caines

Mask me and calmly wall me in
with the lean thief who spies and eyes
and the one who claws, lusts to rape –
a cursed rebellion. Nurseries
will face the wall; children will gag
their dolls in preparation for
the trial. Under a botched tree,
my enemies will tongue of war

and prayerpiece out some words,
will lip and mouth. Some sacrifice
will ape the braying myths they trumpet,
while their bloat general lies
in his cups, calling them to armour,
to gather beneath the braced oak
and countenance – scholar and dunce
and fundamentalist alike –

the chance to brain men such as me.
Perhaps these fine examiners
may grin broadly and hide their grief
at this. One lashes Belladonna,
who, exculpated, suffers still,
although it is not him she eyes
but certain, better-looking others.
And when one lashes, still one lies.

I speak of this, and greater losses,
coming around the abject curve.
I try to mouth prophetic words.
I'm silenced, masked in a sleeve.

Ah – Mr Thomas!

I . . . must apologise. And I hope you might contemplate forgiving this desperate act of chummying up – again! But the thing is, I've gone and filched some nouns of yours – again – this time from 'O make me a mask' – and set myself a pointless challenge: write a poem (or verses if not a poem, but let's not go there, if you please) that use those particular words in that particular order – but as *verbs* rather than *nouns*. That's all – a pointless piece of self-constraint. Do you mind?

The point is, that is, the point really is: this is merely the most pointless outbreak yet of my constant *puzzling* about you. And maybe this puzzling isn't dazzlingly welcome. I do assure you, though: these are strange times, and you come strangely to mind now more than ever before.

So – I hope you won't mind. I hope you won't mind. (I was not far from Milkwood Road in Herne Hill in south-west London, the other day, and . . . but never mind. Here we are.) Here you are, on the shelf, in the heart, on the tongue – in the mind.

Good night, Mr Thomas. Good night –
Michael

Dancing at Bar Inbhir Èireann – Eileen Carney Hulme

I am thirty on this shore
alone with the waves and the blue
and the pull of light
druids divining
butterflies sleeping
barefoot I am singing summer
as October rises
from a birch tree
like a glory moth seeking heaven.

D

Who knew we share a birthday month and I always write a poem for myself in October.

Never managed seven stanzas though so here's my one stanza effort.

Perhaps in another time, another place we might have raised a glass or two.

Cheers

E

Littlestone – A C Clarke

I was young and free and happy as the sea was wide
the beach stretching for miles combed into permanent waves
the dunes a tumble of sift that I scrambled
shoes full of sand,
too eager for seashells and castle-building to mind
the stiff-bladed marram, alert for the turn of the tide.

I was light I was easy blown by a wind from the south
my feet flew over the pavements like leaves in a skitter of rain
I had castles to build, cockles to dig for
pink sticks of rock
to suck to stumps tacky as fly-paper, candyfloss
to smear into my mouth.

Oh all those hours and days of a calm
we never found elsewhere.
Even now I remember
only sunshine and twilit hours so clear
you could just make out the lights of Cap Gris Nez
as the white-coifed sea chanted its evening psalm.

When I went back the weather had turned.
Clouds banked to the west. Out on the ness
cooling-towers overlooked the shingle and seagrass,
our road a ribbon of new-builds,
a blaze of light drowning the starmilk sky.
And where was the child who had built out of sand?

Dear Dylan

Forgive my nerve in pastiching the opening line of my favourite poem of yours. *Fern Hill* is so buoyantly alive!

You wouldn't have much truck with the 'well-made poem' which is like a taxidermist's prize specimen, carefully sewn together out of dead matter. Of course I'm offering a hostage to fortune here. I'm not pretending that I've ever had your sheer verve and dazzle, your sleight of tongue, your mouth-music. Rap would be more your style today than the mimsier products of creative writing courses. Too bad!

I just want you to know that *Fern Hill* has enchanted me since the day I read it, at the same age as the mythic number of your whiskies, and its last lines have held me from my green to my winter days.

However thin my voice, I hope to sing in my chains till the death of my time.

Yours,
Anne

Laugharne 68 – Rachael Clyne
with lines from Dylan Thomas

A pair of armchairs serve as garnitures for the mantelpiece,
with its flat-back dogs and electric fire. Outside,
the Tâf estuary pales into cawl as rain settles in.

A child's rocking-chair, maybe Aeronwy's, squats like a pet
next to a velvet chaise. Chatter drifts up from below,
where visitors tuck into bara brith and welsh cakes.

From the wireless on the corner cupboard, his voice
booms out each syllable of *ffish-wiffe* and *re-lig-i-on*,
trumpeting the place where fish spool in the hooting, leery dark2

An ageing English plonks himself on the chaise, while his wife
explores the house. *It's the stairs,* he explains. *I'd like to say
it's because of coalmining, but really it was years of smoking.*

Man be my metaphor…broken ghosts with glow worms in their heads.

Now the room is full. A man with rucksack and wife
with large umbrella, fiddle with phones that chime alerts.
We all chat over Dylan's continuous incantations.

*… their bones under the windings of the sea….and death shall have no
dominion…*

I imagine the Bakelite phone ring. A hand takes the receiver
and with a voice like *the force that through the green fuse
drives the flower*, declares, *Laugharne 68, Dylan speaking.*

Dear Dylan

I visited your home the other day and found it an amiable abode.

It appears to be as you left it, although I doubt they were your actual undergarments hanging on the line outside. The complexities of your domestic arrangements were discretely documented in folders.

The kitchen now offers refreshments to the crowds of visitors, who paw through your memorabilia. Your sonorous voice continues to broadcast through the wireless and you have retained your telephone number.

Today's estate agents declare that location is all and I cannot imagine a more poetic spot than the Boathouse, with its estuary vista and harr. How wise to have a separate writing shed, a brief walk away.

You transported us with your lyrical language and relish of human character in everyday life. *Under Milk Wood* became a favourite with amateur dramatic societies. Your lines and phrases have gained a memorable place in our literature.

I shall give it a five-star review on Trip Advisor.

Rachael

Laugharne by Night – Paul Deaton

The day bleeds out.
We really don't know what to do.
The clock tower has told the same time for a hundred years.
The jackdaws spiral. Spring
from a spine of brittle winter trees.
Altogether. Electro-convulsed.
Life. A long random series of shock treatments.
They're all a' japes. Scruffy jacketed comrades
catching a collective cold.
Darkness descends. The day's crypt.
One street leads up. The other down.
Evening's High Noon.
All front doors are shut.
They'll always be locked in your life.
Always barred for the final showdown.

We wander to the crumbling castle,
looking like a half-eaten wedding cake.
Lover, where did all the party guests go?
Surfeit of stars. Increase in the night stream.
Betelgeuse blinging-it,
winks out a warm orange strobe.
Would we be happier there?
The whole finger-pointed asterism,
a starfish stuck, no thrown, to Carmarthen's cellar ceiling.
We head home from our late hour saunter.
The bed cast up, also thrown,
waits wantonly, a flotsam raft
from what went down,
and the two of us,
our lone lives now, strangely surfaced.

Postcard to Dylan

Laugharne Spring 1949

Pawned or penniless,
whatever you do, Dylan,
Wales is waiting for you.

p.s. a starch stiff letter from a J.M. Brinnin,
USA stamp, franked New York,
I've left, tilted, top-shelf, behind the bar at Brown's.

Plus a get started cheque.

The Boat House keys, beneath these.

M.T.

Today waits – Olga Dermott-Bond

Bright morning billows in a blue-boat sky;
the back garden is singing sparrow-bright,
A high-thrown salt smell of the near lough
is scattered to the back door of mum's
kitchen. Inside,
                    my daughters sleep
slack-armed, headlong against light,
precious fig hearts ripening inside
too-hot pyjamas. In a hall cupboard
dad's red coat waits for him to return,
friendly ghosts of hankies in the pockets
crumpled with laughter.
                            Mum's hearing aids
curl, baby seahorses, beside her bed, blinking
in shallow pools that eddy yellow through
a muffled curtain patch; bones behind
her ears clever skeletons who want only
to rest in peace, not be a-jangle with
second parts of sentences, starts of words
soft as baby's skin. Moving
                                outside, I am
bare-footed, bone-shriek-cold. Loosening
the washing line I string it up, crow-high,
over the house. I step into this shuddering
balance, a tightrope from yesterday to today,
pulled far between strong branches still green
with grief. I breathe in fields and closed bibles
of unripe blackberries: far below,
                                    I see every
inch. Today waits to be shelled all over again,
like love. Today, shiny-squeaky, small and pure
and simple as a pea, split from a pod.

Dear Dylan,

I was wondering what your greatest regret was? I don't have many, but there is one I'd like to confess to you. Let me set the scene...

It was my school production of *Under Milk Wood*, on closing night. The dusk was falling around Llareggub, the narrowness of students' bodies safety-pinned into tweed waistcoats, frown lines painted on their young faces. I realised my regret when Reverend Jenkins was giving his blessing at sundown. I hadn't asked my Dad to come. (He wasn't very well by then).

Standing in the wings I knew that he would have loved it; each letter steamed open, each daydream caught. A year later he was gone. Now every time I hear the prayer of your play I feel the soft-sharp pull and push of love and loss. It is, 'all at once night now', and there is no bringing him back.

Perhaps I am like Captain Cat, dreaming of the dead who want still so much to be alive, alive, alive...

Yours,
Olga

Poem inspired by *'Under Milk Wood'* *"...this place of love..."*

The Gravity of Missing – Kitty Donnelly

A heron sifts the Calder with his eye,
and drizzle turns on the wind like a lashing

till the coal-face of the valley hardens, stooping
to survey this grief that wears her heels

with pacing miles and miles of absence,
as though measuring sorrow by distance.

A train passes, giddy with light.
Night pools by the foxgloves, untenanted.

If she crosses the packhorse bridge, entering
the hood of trees, there might be answers –

or above where the Pleiades flee Orion's pursuit
through a fire of constellations, respite

from intractable words tossed from the tongue,
this slow canal, these aching feet, the gravity of *missing*.

Dear Dylan,

I'm sorry we didn't meet in Laugharne. I mispronounced the name of the town and the bus driver – after having a good, lilting laugh at my stupidity – purposefully dropped me in Llanybri instead. I can see you smiling at your usual table in Brown's.

Anyway, I spent the afternoon in *The Farmer's Arms* talking to the landlady and reading *Death's and Entrances.* A storm came on late in the afternoon and I see now how this landscape is the very soul of your poetry, its pulse.

Of course I have heard the rumours, but I'm not much interested in gossip. Anything of meaning to me will come from your own pen.

I eventually made it to Laugharne, one particularly vicious December day. By then you were long gone, but I walked along the shoreline and thought of you a great deal, wishing our paths had crossed.

Yours faithfully,
Kitty

Laugharne – Matt Duggan

I woke in the birth of darkest morning
Sound of a pony's hooves scraping against granite;

Following the forest to a road of open borders
Guarded by rooks that thread the castle remains.
I walk the shill of black air – sills of light
Like children jumping for a higher shelf;
Peaking bright pockets of sun crowning the morning
with the crispy repeats of dew.

Reaching an ivy smouldered cabin
window smeared with an amber moss
writing desk levelled to a vista of trickling water
a pen cushioned in inkling ash;

a morning in black hoods of cloud
where a moon lights up a castle like a cathedral;
I saw discarded fishing wrecks sleeping in dribbles
simmered by a slow tide of blue and wide sparks.

Dear Dylan,

If it wasn't for Mr Ford my secondary school English teacher I wouldn't be writing today, as he read us stories and poems that enthralled us all about your life and reputation, and then read your words in front of us,

If it wasn't for the poems I read I'd never had met my partner who I passed pencilled square slices of paper jotted with lines from your poems over a sticky bar every Friday night.

It was you Dylan, who brought us together when we walked along the paths of Laugharne to the watering holes in New York.

It was you who inspired me to write every-day.

Thank you
Matt

How many ways can you describe the sun? – Barry Fentiman Hall

An orange for the half time sugar,
sucked between puffs of an old sweet smoke.

A tomato getting old and sagging from the weight of its own heat
squashing into the bottom of a greasy pan.

A cold slab fish eye looking blankly,
codlike from April afternoon skies, grey light hardly felt.

Fried egg like a child would paint,
perfect round and not yet broken, pink over easy lollipop trees.

Dirty red death penny for the eyes of the departed.
Brother, mother, other, gone.

A carnelian stone set in a king's seal
Cut and polished with the authority of a poet.

Inspired by *"Who do you wish was with us?"* from *'Portrait of the Artist as a Young Dog'*

Dear Dylan

I thought you were dead. It says so in the history books and them films on the BBC. Then this lad came in The Cross House bold as muck, and he was the spit of you. Face like cheese and a gob like raspberries.

He said he'd come to sign up for the slam. Funny thing is with the clothes he was wearing he fitted right in with the young lads and lasses doing all the shouting and such. And he spoke very well he did, all that stuff about death and the green of the grass. He didn't win mind,

But it was nice to see for all that. He was your ghost I suppose? Or just some actor?

I don't know how this letter will reach you Dylan Voice, but since you're dead and you made me up I reckon there's always a chance, what with me being a postman and all. Me and the missus never did those things you said we did by the way, but never mind that now.

May the tea be strong wherever you may be.

Yours
W. Nilly

Tentacles and Tar – Caroline Gill

A sailor's song lies buried in Doom Bar
beneath the jellyfish and rolling waves;
but will it rise through tentacles and tar?

Escape means danger and a battle scar:
it envies porpoises who risk close shaves.
A sailor's song lies buried in Doom Bar

despite its urge to crown a schooner's spar
with ropes and rigging for its shanty staves.
But will it rise through tentacles and tar?

It feels as safe as roe in caviar
and must break out of Davy Jones's graves.
A sailor's song lies buried in Doom Bar,

where there is neither moon nor brittlestar:
its music pulses through the sandbank caves,
but will it rise through tentacles and tar?

The porpoises sense rhythms from afar,
and dive to snout out underwater raves.
A sailor's song lies buried in Doom Bar,
but will it rise through tentacles and tar?

Written in response to *'Ears in the turrets hear'*

Dear Dylan,

Son of the wave, your voice still ripples in, ruffling the blue-glass basin of Swansea Bay. An old sea captain leans out over the South Dock, watching with his inner eye for a turning of the tide, his ears of bronze ever open to those possibilities that stretch before us all on horizons that are nearly out of reach.

Like you, I lived high above the shore in my crow's nest home; but unlike you, I hardly ever woke to a white Christmas. Just occasionally a flurry of flakes would nestle in my latticed window: there was one memorable morning when the fringe of the ocean sparkled with stars of ice.

Number 5 stands very much as it stood in those youthful days when you ran wild with *mitching* friends. I sat in your parents' parlour some years ago, sensing the torrents of words that whistled round in your head, soaring, fluttering and falling in tandem with the October leaves.

Months later, I chased your shadow round the tulip beds under the cherry trees in Cwmdonkin Park, pausing by the pool to wonder what further fountains might, just might, have overflowed from the nib of your pen ...

Yours,
Caroline

One year in Penperlleni – Ronnie Goodyer

Living alone in the rambling manse, post divorce,
poetry arrived in many forms and for one year
that form was three men, a Ruth and two Maggies.
Never our own poems, always our own choices.
Sylvia and Emily, Ezra and Auden,
T.S. E and Dylan T, with Dylan the only constant.

Outside, we were the boys and girls of summer,
blowing laughter clouds over my chunk of Penperlleni hill.
Inside, when cold blew the valley and the east wind chilled,
we were fire-flicker-cushioned for the warmth of poetry
in deep nights of words, Rioja and perfumed smoke.

On Dylan-Only nights we fell into forms as months grew:
Philip was master of the strident and the rousing,
I was the one for the gentler colours and country sleeping,
Ruth was responsible for the death of a child and genesis.
Maggie 1 and Maggie 2 were listeners on these nights,
but hopelessly wonderful John always entertained
with mispronunciations, his own random flow and fall.

When the last embers crackled goodnight,
when our stanzas were bruised in oratory
or conversations descended to happy-trash,
we'd retire to beds, to reassemble over
unsubdued breakfast and arrange the day.
Maybe later, a taxi down the road to Abergavenny
for a quieter poetry night at the Hen and Chicks.

Dear Dylan

I was 10, at the funeral of a relation I'd never heard of. At the wake, one person from each table (I didn't know any of them) stood and said something about the deceased. It was so BOR-ing. That was until one man rose, stayed silent for about ten seconds, and then – *"AND DEATH SHALL HAVE NO DOMINION..."*

He talked about wind, moon, stars, and the sea. And that first line was gnawing into my brain. I'd heard nothing like it before, and I loved it. I asked dad what 'dominion' meant and was told to shush. I plucked up courage to ask the man what he'd read. He wrote a name on his napkin, told me to take it to the library and ask if they'd let me borrow it, as it wasn't in the children's section. A week later I was reading *'Collected Poems'*.

I couldn't understand the poems, but picked the words which shone for me. I was lost in this. I wrote favourite words and phrases in my rough book to memorise.

That was many years ago and your words have stayed throughout my life, even changed it. They've given me many happy times, on my own and with company. I wanted to thank you but have not had the chance until now.

So, as the 10 year old me would have said, "Thank you, Mr Thomas." Or, if I may, "Thank you, Dear Dylan."

Ronnie

Portrait of a Friend – John Greening

Three times the grey seal
'bottles' – a dog's head
taking a breather –
before it vanishes under
milk and honey Gower
in search of wilder headlands.

Time enough for new worlds,
late play, balancing
accounts, a Marina,
and for that net of surf
to baffle the brains as I push
through hart's-tongue and sycamore

a third time. Like a seal
breaking, I read into every
mummified shag or shining
foal on the shore a sense
that I am poking my head into
something briefly miraculous.

Dear Dylan

You may be surprised that my poem doesn't focus on you. It's not that I don't admire your work. *'Do not go gentle into that good night'* is one of the great formal elegies and, had you written nothing else, your name would be remembered like Chidiock Tichbourne's for a single masterpiece.

There are two or three other fine achievements in verse, too. Then there's *Under Milk Wood* , one of those works that feels as if it has always existed, detached from its creator, like the *Unfinished Symphony.*

But where would you have been without your friend, Vernon Watkins? And have you ever considered how shabbily you treated him, even failing to turn up as his Best Man. Didn't he do all your typing for you? He certainly lent you money (and a suit) and selected your memorial stone, as commemorated in his *'At Cwmrhydyceirw Quarry'.*

You weren't always generous about those poems ("too obviously written in words") though you had more in common than you'll admit, especially (as your friend pointed out in his introduction to the letters you sent him – naturally you didn't keep his!) a religious instinct and suspicion of "a poem dominated by time".

I hope he's still looking after you.

Yours,
John

Cubicles of You – Lois Hambleton

Cubicles of you within my bones, the blood, the sinew
a stirring in the tongue of limbs and toes,
the purring earth as primal milk unfolds.
The juice of Eve, it trickles, turns to seeping
primed and targeted upon the birth of you.

No antidote against the cells of womb and wildness
advancing from the bluebells and the scattering seed,
the brown ploughed fields of ache and longing.
My son, you did not tread in spring, you came today
and chose a cradle leafed in bloodied warmth.

You sparkled where the swifts had fled the rain
and autumn sought with giant, orange hands
the gathering bloom of beast and grain.
It was for me, the harvest hymn of birthdays
singing with the apples and the ripening hues of home.

Inspired by' *Poem in October'*

Dear Dylan,

I am compelled to write upon this day, the birthday of my youngest son and you. What greater time for inspiration? He works abroad this year but will raise a pint to you with evening meal, America has beckoned as it did for you, some similarities here I feel.

I found a photograph of me today posing in the doorway of the Boathouse. I was young and thrilled to be where you had lived. A local fisherman was showing visitors through empty rooms and although the writing shed was bare, I saw you, looking out across the sea, a bottle of beer in hand and a well-worn pencil resting on one ear. Just as poetry ought to be.

When I'm stuck with life and writing, I have an Englishman, an Irishman and a Welshman to refer my issues to. Shakespeare for insight and meaning, Oscar Wilde for flamboyance, and you, for words and lyricism, and wildness. All my life I have dwelled in the pages of your collected poems. I read *Newquay* if I want to laugh and *Fern Hill*, if I need to cry.

I hope this finds you on a higher tide, will write again next October.

Yours as ever …
Lois

The Green Fuse – Adam Horovitz

I never really learned to sing.
My childhood was subsumed instead
by the subtle music of words. I swam
amongst deft rhymes (Charles Causley,
Laurie Lee), echoed my father's joyful
chants and blissful nonsense games.

At school, the other children said
I couldn't hold a tune. I took
their word for it, but followed
my mother's voice home
through the woods; each syllable
as bright as one of Hansel's stones.

Meaning came to me slowly, as if
I was learning to speak over and over,
my tongue a trap for the cadences
of living. I copied everything
but the tunes that came simply
to other tongues.

Yes I was young and easy, in love
with the sounds of the spring;
my mouth an echoing cave
inhabited by straws of verse.
I was ripe for the voice of a Welsh man
caught in a wheel of wax; ready

to be driven through his green fuse
beyond the need for song.

Dear Dylan,

I write this from the edge of hearing, from the doorway of a poetry reading, listening (as you listened) to 'the shape and shade and size and noise' of words.

The room is quiet, but the world is loud. Time stutters as the poet's voice rises up from a tinny microphone. His words hum, strum, jig and gallop out into the porous street. Who knows what the poet is saying. Right now, it doesn't matter. Verses run down his chin like juice from some vulgar orange, escape him utterly. They ooze out into the half-dark, seep down rhyming cracks in the pavement, pool in assonant shop doorways.

The structure of his words is written in streetlights, in the sighs and curses of late night drunkards, in the echoing refrains of the wind. The poet's voice is cut down, sampled, sped up and mixed with the beat of lives beyond his words. His poems are liberated from sense.

Nothing goes gentle into this cacophonous night. The poet's voice swoops off like seagulls after chips. Meaning rides the tongue of the tide, morphs into music. Understanding is for the slow processes of morning.

In this moment, however, I am ecstatically yours,
Adam

When We Met – Elizabeth Horrocks

You were my own discovery, Dylan.
I was seven when you died,
far from our land which you loved and hated,
far too soon for you to be thought respectable,
or studied at school.

But when I was fifteen, I bought your play for voices.
I was on holiday from my sea city,
neighbour and rival to your "lovely, ugly town".
Had left for a while its gleaming white buildings
and dirty, decaying docks.

Under the shadow of a North Wales castle
I opened the book and sat, enchanted,
as boats bustled past, or called in the quayside.
But none were called Zanzibar
or Star of Wales.

And the lilt of the language,
the rhythm of the sloeblack, slow, black,
crowblack, fishingboat-bobbing sea,
and the humour, the warmth, the sharp eye,
entranced and inspired.

I have loved you ever since.

Dear Dylan,

As you can see from the poem, I have been a fan of yours since 1963. Like you I am Welsh. I live in England, as you did for a time, and although I love my life here, sometimes hiraeth sweeps over me, mainly for the rhythms and cadences of Wales, for the sheer loquacity of its people, for the joy in words and language that my fellow countrymen and women have, speaking the language of the neighbouring English, who often do not seem to appreciate the wonder of their own tongue.

And then I can listen to Under Milk Wood, or to you, reading A Child's Christmas in Wales, or the marvellous August Bank Holiday, or indeed any of your pieces – drama, prose or poetry – and I can be emotional, like any true Celt and so restore my equilibrium.

Thank you.
Elizabeth

& this is where Dylan was – Mab Jones
Written during a residency in the Dylan Thomas Boathouse

& this is where Dylan was;
& this is the armchair his oncebody
sat in; & here is a curl from
the crest of his hair; & this is a tooth
of his, brown from boiled sweets;
& here is the rug edge where tipsy
he tumbled, onto the floorboards
unpolished as truth; & here is the letter
he wrote to his mother; & here is the answer
though crumbled to dust.

                    Look, here's
the sink that his hands sometimes doved in,
washing the ink from his thumb like
a saint; & here is the fireplace which
warmed his brown toenails, & this is a
clipping turned silver with age. Here
is a pinch of his mossy tobacco,
& here is a thread from his best Sunday
shirt. & here is a scrap of a pillow
he lay on, & here is an eyelash,
& here is some dirt which he swept
from his leg when he sat at a reading
of Under Milk Wood in New York.
& here is his fork. & here is an
ember, from his front fireplace
which raged for a while
then went dark.

Dearest Dyl,

I'm sure you would be interested to know that there's now a day each year in your honour. I ran International Dylan Thomas Day for two years. it takes place on May 14th, which is the date of the first ever public reading of Under Milk Wood.

Yes, you belong to the world, now, not just to Wales. During the last Dylan Day I ran there were 62 events in your honour, in places as diverse as Patagonia and Portugal.

You are as international as Coca Cola, Dylan my dear. You are as everyday as soap. Your fans have clubs all across the earth, and your poems are included in Hollywood films. I'm sure your toes will twinkle when you learn of this.

Your old writing shed, which Caitlin used to lock you in sometimes, is now like a religious sanctum, and people visit from all around the world. We open it only on special occasions. All your things are covered in the most glorious dust, like relics. You're talked about as if you're a saint! You naughty old sinner you. I'm sure you must be quite delighted.

With love, and best wishes,
Mab

The weight and wonder of words – Roy McFarlane

All poets must carry an Akua'ba
because they desire to become pregnant
with words, to birth fully formed words
and informed words because words
are never deformed; constantly growing,
evolving, shaping, taking on and taking off.

Yes, all poets like the Akan-speaking
Nations of Ghana, should carry small,
flat wooden dolls inscribed with words,
blessed by the priestess of poetry.

Yes, all poets should carry them
in the bloom of the moon or the turn
of the sun, tucked inside jackets,
into waist sash, under vest close to the heart.

Yes, words should always be washed,
fed and always given matching ear-rings.

Dear Dylan,

"Roistering, drunken and doomed poet," I'm not sure where I found these words but what a quote, my friend, I call you my friend because your poems and the craft of writing have found me - *for the raging moon I write.*

I've learned about your creative process, being locked away in that shed in Wales, scrapping and scratching, muttering and mumbling, intoning and changing words. This revelation means so much to me, the weight of a word, the metronome existence in the centre, oh my god, I want a shed, I want a space, I want all the time to ruminate into existence a word – *exercised in the still night.*

Glyn Maxwell a poet you'd love, seeks meaning in words and space, seriously space on the page, the white space, every word and white space earning it's right on the page. And I guess death (one of your favourite subjects) is that space around us, our companion, our ever-present friend to write into, live into and to love between those spaces. This is a letter to you my friend, and a gift called the Akua'ba for the eternal you – *labouring by the singing light.*

Yours
Roy

Swansong – Nicholas McGaughey

After the leaves left, a chill wind came
with a day to blow in my hometown.
It was a cold return to places that had gone,
to remain a different city.

The castle's skull still stared over the ruins
of my last engagement, lost in a parade
of banks prinked into bars and quick hotels.
I hit the new low of High Street,

scrawled and boarded, crawling meekly
to the white hope of the station; buddleias sprouted
from the cornerstones of proud institutions,
the pubs I chopsed in, muffled long ago.

I pictured the snow and a full moon of crosses
like footprints over roofs and pavements,
the silver birds with tongues of fire. And all the bells
not ringing, with news of somewhere else.

Inspired by the Radio Play 'Return Journey'

Dear Dylan,

I had a day off in Swansea last week...I saw your name and face everywhere but I couldn't find you at all. The Mermaid was a block of flats. The Three Lamps, The Number 10 all gone with the slops into the Tawe.

The Kardomah has moved lock stock and coffee pot four streets from where it steamed. And Duw Duw! What have they done to old Wind Street eh? All the banks are pubs and knocking shops! And the women with almost nothing on, on a Sunday..afternoon! With the boys dribbling behind them all stalk-eyed with bad intentions and betting slips!!

Old Swansea is dead like you said. What the planes didn't do for, we did and time took, and all the people went in cars to retail parks and drank at home and made the town a place of ghosts, with the past nailed away behind the planks that board the pubs up. I bet if I jemmied any of them open I'd hear you at the bar giving it large...!

Anyway, when you get this, drop the fiver off at the Queens, ...The barmaids are nice there...it must be worth £50 now.

Don't Tell The Wife,
Jones

Twenty Can't be Carved on Any Stone – Jenny Mitchell

The priest spoke over me at first, loud
with the last rites, robes like wings at ease.
I whispered: *Son, you shan't be self-destroyed.*
Twenty can't be carved on any stone.

Your upturned face sought no reflection
in the ceiling till I raised my voice:
You will not leave me childless in this room.
Twenty can't be carved on any stone.

When breathing stopped, the *beep* gained
speed as the priest looked down, book closed.
He shook his head; gave up the ghost.
Twenty can't be carved on any stone.

I screamed *Come back,* and took your hand.
The priest intoned: *God gives and takes away.*
You heard me say: *Too soon,* squeezed back.
Twenty can't be carved on any stone.

Inspired by *'Do Not Go Gentle into That Goodnight'*

Dear Dylan – must I call you Mr Thomas?

Is it true about the chair? Did you really saw the legs? Was that cutting down to raise you up, or just a tipsy joke? I mean, you can't believe what people say.

Television is a village filled with chat, septic in the throat, spewed out. Is that all it was – their base defilement? They cannot hurt you much with stories of your married life, the drink. Poets of the old school lurched from one pub to the next. It was how they found their inspiration, something of the sort.

But to cut the legs – that makes you a patriarch. How could words as passionate as yours fly from a pettifogging heart? It wasn't wrong to have a woman keep your house. You caroused with stars; Richard Burton talks about you well on *Parkinson*.

But did you really cut whole inches off the chair so the char would sit beneath you as she took your orders? Where's the poetry in that? Surely some mistake, reported on the BBC to lower your good name. I wish you'd speak, send word they're wrong.

Dear Mr Thomas, please, be Dylan once again.

Best Wishes,
Jenny

Millennial Borders – Rufus Mufasa

My borderline Cockett/Town Hill make shift
Home for now, schooling some things I don't want
No more Mumbles, it belongs to childhood.

Telecommunications industry
Buildings of businessmen, steroids and speed
My borderline Cockett/Town Hill make shift.

The Palace, class A's – back then I danced Rave
Escape DJ's salaried alongside
No more Mumbles, it belongs to childhood.

Top Banana to avoid the Come Down
Dai Flies swiped my Purple Haze down The Dunes
My borderline Cockett/Town Hill make shift.

Chav meets David Evans and Habitat
Bong Shops every corner, Mix for super
No more Mumbles, it belongs to childhood.

Clutch control freeriding blue Fiesta
Every pay day sale rail, party bigger
My borderline Cockett/Town Hill make shift
No more Mumbles, it belongs to childhood.

Dearest Dylan,

I need your help. How do I make it stop? How do you readjust to home with a brain-full of rolling marbles, big bowling balls, rioting for full attention, demanding to be decoded, poisoning me to process; the chat of the Indonesian kitten, too tiny to be away from mam, eyes not even open, scrounging for catfish guts...how to decipher that milkless message? How to scribe the divine diction of a dog?

Dylan, it can't be right to see your toddler cut the baby's hair and read that as an their innate tribal ceremonial understanding, a fully formed poem unfolding...
I'm nostalgic for my children, especially when away working, but I'm not sure I'm fully present when I return, with an unexplainable obligation to scribe my eyes on the world...

Dylan, I don't have a shed. I don't even have a proper desk. I do most of my work in my bed, which translates as resting, or worse, lazy, and not where a mother should be.
Send some advice for my heart, my pen, my soul and psyche... how to allow it at all, and equally, how to leave it all be.

Forever yours,
Rufus

Weeping willow – Marcelle Newbold

The boy wanted to know so they embraced.
Her bark softened to his apples and knobbles,
less agitated now her tendril jewels dripped.

She did not answer. Although her roots sang
again again and a leaf, perfect in its death,
kissed the frigid ripples to life.

They whispered soundless love: conceived
sinew; osmosis; their thirst. Dreamt indigo sweet
blooms, beds of white, held solace in their skins.

He knew: the full moon flooded her, bled
potential. Death score times score, now a feast
for the roses, evidence of a scheme.

She knew: memory as a trick, there's only now.
So they bathe, drink, exert, worship - keep not to
themselves and believe in divine cultivation.

.

Dear Dylan

I visited the Boat House today and its environs, and on return felt obliged to write immediately to express how the place was thronging and the noise deafening: with popping lugworms, scurrying crabs, languishing seaweed and the permanent rushing of the breeze from goodness knows where to my-good-self.

With the addition of an invasive metronome of a gregarious song thrush plus family, it was impossible not to be confronted with the fact, that here, nature is indeed in command.

At the property itself, the view was breath taking (not a welcome addition after so many steps), and I was also met with what can only be described as an over abundant fig tree. The air was thick with unseasonal sun and the butterflies swarmed like wasps, curtailing my visit.

During my hasty departure the ambiance was once again interrupted by the gushing of a tidal argument, between none less than three estuarial flows. One can only assume this was to serve as a reminder of our fleeting touch within this life - reassuring that 'it' remains constant, whether 'we' are present or not.

I hope next time we correspond it will be under less dramatic circumstances.

Yours faithfully,
Marcelle

By The Writing Shed at Laugharne – Caleb Parkin

File through the flesh where no flesh decks the bones.
        Dylan Thomas, "Light Breaks Where No Sun Shines"

A great jellyfish loiters beneath the surface:
collapsed cathedral dome of its body frayed by estuary.
Un-living water, neither fresh, nor salty, nor brackish;
water which once had fierce appetites. Now
shredding like cellophane, popped
like a dot of bubble-wrap.

Absent from this shed for months, Dylan sweated
at a makeshift office in Tehran: fired off love letters
which may or may not have been read, lost scripts
for the Anglo-Iranian Oil Company, mining the poetics
of petrochemicals. How could he know these layers of ghosts
from the ground would come back to haunt us –
a rising terror in degrees, of incremental returns to sender?

Now in the shed there's a staged desk, scraps of phoney drafts,
above an aptly tattered rug. Below, the jellyfish drifts
through its flotsam afterlife, its skyward shadow
iridescent as a slick.

Hi Dylan,
(Excuse the informality; I send a lot of emails.)

We visited your writing shed not long ago, the wide estuary
bawling out to mysterious shadows on the horizon.
Instead of poetry, I'd like to talk about something even less sexy:
sustainability. It's hard to sustain a living, hard to sustain
relationships – and hard to sustain your writing. Maybe we can't
do all three.

I read about that strange blip on your timeline, the trip to Iran –
and your letters to Caitlin. From the filthy rich elites and the filthy
streets, it sounds like all you could think about was whether love
would sustain. Can anything that fiery keep on burning, even in a
distant desert?

As I write, I'm one year older than you made it to – and
absolutely nowhere near as famous, or as good. Sometimes I wish I
was as intense, as visionary, as you. At others, I'm glad to swerve
that, instead being relatively low maintenance.

In my poem, there's a dead jellyfish near your writing shed,
adrift in the everyday grey of the estuary: which one of us is it?

Tepidly Yours,
Caleb

Dylan and me – Jeff Phelps

Curly-headed and savage
he led me out from school that morning
as Sketty bells churned for mitching
and the Head called 'Boys! Hey, boys.
Where d'you think you're going?'
'We're off to play billiards. Any objections?'
Cut-glass consonants and vowels like plums
his poems in school mags up the secret stairs
in the library. We laughed all the way
to high tide on a worm's head.

My father feared him like the devil
as if his commie alky arrogance could
rub off on me, turn me flabby-jowled
and poetic. And all of it, Welsh lies and legend
lathered through the bottom of a Brains bitter glass,
he pencilled himself in margins
in a beer-matted chicken-boned boathouse.

Still I wish I'd met him that day at Caswell
with Pamela when they walked barefoot
over the oyster-mouthed and scalloped sand
a conscious Woodbine in his hand.
How I would have stared at their brazen
London swagger. Though I wasn't even born
yet I would have warned him of the ending
already rhymed, the penny-grabbing,
hand-to-mouthing, sweet-lipped sophomores
and whisky chasers that would leave him
half a life unwritten, lily-livered,
rascally young and murmuring at us
only to love the words.

Hello Dylan,

Most of the teachers in your old school were afraid of you even after you'd gone: bad influence, no-good-boyo. Somewhat of an embarrassment. You would have laughed. Your life and mine never quite crossed.

They rebuilt your grammar school on the hill and I started there ten years after you died. If poetry was learning Keats and Shelley by heart I hated it. Then one day Wasky wrote the whole of Fern Hill up on the blackboard. You wouldn't have known Wasky – one of the more enlightened English teachers. He led us through it word by word, phrase by phrase. It was subversive stuff. That was when I got poetry. It was a window opening. I was snatched into your swallow-thronged loft.

Then I knew it was possible to be a poet, that poetry was a living thing. You had been to this place and the ink was still wet on your words.

So I want to thank you. You haven't always been an easy friend and I know reliability was never your strong suit. But your words are trustworthy and lasting. I'm certain of that.

Cheers for now.
Your friend,
Jeff

The Three Robbers – David Punter

The robbers came down from the bright hills this morning,
they bore skillets of silver and helmets of gold.
They were dressed all prepared for another day's dawning
when the truth may be honoured and memories sold.

There were three of them glimmering above the high passes
and one had no eyes and another no limbs
and the third held on firm to his grey falcon's jesses,
his tears overflow, and his cup always brims,

Tonight they'll make merry on partridge and pheasant,
they'll call for old brandy and sup of the vine
for their manners are noble, their talk always pleasant,
their oaths are robust and their bridles are fine.

And I would be gone with the robbers tomorrow
up hill and through dale, through enclosure and town
but their tracks are pursued by an inconstant sorrow
that blights all their deeds, brings the grey falcon down.

And so I shall set out myself in the morning
on a skeleton horse with a fox for my friend,
despite all the hubbub, the terrible warning
I shall find my own way through the hills to the end.

After [a long way after] *'I see the boys of summer'*

Dylan *bach*,

In Wales, I am, like you, but not *of* Wales, in love with plangent flow, mutterings of old stooped women on Carmarthen market, and also now the most flamboyant prophet-transvestite you never saw that windowed month of Swansea-cold Methodist Sundays, my people were Ystwyth valley lead-miners, you know, in Pontrhydygroes at beck of Lisburne's absent earl, then dead before thirty, heritaged now, their green life ebbed, death heath hearth, and I wrote a visit yesterday (Welsh cousins are all yesterday):

Stiff over coffee we were, in our raincoats,
Hefyn, our host, legs deep-scarred,
known all over, used to be
the newsagent, everybody knows
Hefyn. And his sister Annie,
silent now, in the deep heart's thrall;
Mary, over eighty, holding things
together, managing cups without a tremor
on which we didn't like to comment.
And Beryl, poor Beryl, shaking
and innocent; but we didn't have
the language, the Welsh tongue
that had contrived all this, like a sonnet
but for us with the wrong words.

I think it's called 'Like a Sonnet', what about you Dylan *bach*? Or maybe 'To these aged girls of winter', but my God, I know how harsh those Welsh winters can be.

David

A bit of a talking to – Terence Quinn

The thing is (*I said*)
is that I think you need
to get a bit of a grip

look at yourselves
heads scrunched together
hidden in these woodlands
year after year
as if you're ashamed
of being seen in simple white

and that's the point
(*raising voice slightly*)
those summer plants are
just plain gaudy
a touch of frost and they're off

you're better than that
you should be proud
not in a boastful way (*I added*)
but I've seen you
fighting your way through snow
living off the land
not needing supplies
Napoleon couldn't do that

So this time next year
it's shoulders back and chins up
(*I gave a demonstration*)
you'd better be out of here.

D,

You seem to be in the middle of even more nowhere than before. Are you heading west. Last night's audience sounded exuberant. I did get a smile out of 'their Moms and Dads were there'. If the poems ever dry up you could do a 'Guide to the Lecture Theatres of the World'.

But more to the point did you sell any books? Don't look at the exchange rate just bring back as many fags and whisky as you can. Have you got the time to do those workshops your man asked about? On balance I think you'd be good at it. The balance being to your bank account - be careful.

I went to see that poet G recommended and wasn't impressed. I think he was trying to be you but with a hat. Which reminds me, I think that if you think about it I did advise you to take an overcoat.

I wrote out 'Poem in October' in a card for my friend's 30th. How many times have I done that. Told her to walk up and down the stairs like I did on mine.

Better go now, time for a Guinness. Jealous?

J

After *'The Force That Through The Green Fuse Drives The Flower'*

A Dream – Anna Saunders

Dylan, I dreamt I was your poem.
Your words wriggled in their genesis
like tadpoles hatching in a stream.

Dylan, I dreamt I was the page,
your starfish-fingers splayed gold upon my skin,
your writing ribboning like bladderwrack.

In a roost as high as a rookery
over an estuary where the mirroring sun spools
you filled me with beak-hard vowels,
consonants soft as the sands.

Every creature asleep,
the rooks in their crowns of thorn,
the gulls on the settled waters

and the night mute of caw or cry,
just your ghost whispering through my lines.

How close we were Dylan,
intimate as only the poet and the poem can be,

your mouth as tight to my page
as the incoming tide to the shore.

Dear Dylan,

What a day for a pilgrimage – the rain didn't stop all afternoon and we arrived late at Laugharne.

Dylan, my father had just died and I was awash with grief, disintegrating in a slow dissolve like the castle walls in the November mist. Everywhere was closing, but we did your birthday walk, climbing the lane through the trees, the bells of the foxgloves chiming with your songs.

Dylan, I felt I belonged there – the Welsh estuary mirroring the platinum planes of my Northern home. I didn't feel alone looking down on the moon-pale shores, with your ghost and my father's intermingling, as the waters spangled in a glitter tide of tears.

Dylan, I am not afraid to say I wept with a double grief, a double homecoming. But my tongue was locked and still like the brackish waters in the oxbow pools.

We arrived late and everything was closing, except my heart Dylan, except my heart.

With love,

Anna x

The Gate – John Sewell

I thought it was a gate you rested your elbow on
in that photo from '52 of you in Laugharne Churchyard.
Dickie-bowed in waist-height undergrowth. Smarter
than your denim Boathouse look. But unsmiling, doleful even.
Beset that summer with yet more tax and rent demands.
Your father dying. You, with just a winter and one summer
left. The poems all out there save the spring-trap rhymes
of *Prologue*, and the *Elegy* unfinished at *the roots of the sea*.

I longed to reach that gate myself, be where you stood,
see what you saw. Those dingled pathways into light
brought days alive in greenfire glory. I kept in every
house I owned, a poster of that photo on my wall -
a prompt, a call, a beckoning. Except the gate
was railings round a grave, and the railings gone
with all the undergrowth. Nothing to rest back against
when finally I found the spot at last.

Trapped there between the graves, you wear the face
of your *Lament*, look out so longingly at what goes on
day in day out, in rooms like mine - loving, living, making do.
As sure as death is sure (your line), that gate won't let you
through to us, or us to you. But it opened free a world
we didn't know was there, with so much upswung heart
moonhid and mute until you nightingaled it round,
netted live as words, a peerless singing firmament.

Inspired by the photo of DT in Laugharne Churchyard, 1952

Dear Dylan,

Why in horror's name go back there a fourth time? America is cruel. It eats its own. Witness the monster it's thrown up lately. Think Goya's *Saturn Devouring His Son*, and give the fiend a bottle-blond comb-over.

Your cache of poems is worth a zillion times what he's slimeballed his way to. That senseless, lonely New York death should be his, not yours.

Enough. I had to get that off my chest, mourn what you might have done if you'd been <u>on</u>, not in, your Laugharne hillside a few years longer.

We owe you such a lot (how's that for a pecuniary turn-around). We who come like tides; leave tracelessly as moonlight.

While you stay ever vital. Walking through the door of Brown's, throwing wide your alliterative arms to cry: *I'm back. Raise a glass.*

Cheers, Dylan, Cheers.
John

After Fern Hill – Penelope Shuttle

Better to live in one of the apple towns
alive
in their windfall light
than in any of these sullen no-hoper postcodes
hosting our screen-sapped days –
to live in that golden world held like an orb of feeling
in his hand,
peaceable kingdom for the poet
dreamy on fern-seed and wordplay
making everything new
till the word grew amazed at itself
saw what it might be
all the moon long
Better for us to live there and not in this fake-world
cursed by and made of liars' looping tongues –
he of the poems holds out a spellbound thread
        take hold
        follow where it leads
to the apple towns and the owls
the swallows over the stables
world as farm
love's starry limits never reached
but stretching further and deeper into the once-only light
matching us step for step
if we care to follow
the thread of his words
bright-whole and undamaged
enduring long past the poet's own brokenness

Dear Dylan,

Now you are dwelling on Parnassus where there are no hangovers! Last week I walked through Lamorna in a dazzle of daffodils and primroses. Soon I came by that low-lying old house where you stayed the night before marrying Caitlin.

She wore a new blue dress, you were in your old corduroys, not a coin in your pocket.

That house was the first in Lamorna to have floorboards. It was built from shipwreck timber in 1868, as was often the Cornish custom.

I remembered Peter telling me of hearing you read as a student at Cambridge, in the Fifties. Your fame came before you. *So how disappointed I was*, Peter said, *when a shabby plump guy with a fag stuck to his lip was introduced... I noted at once a pronounced lack of charisma in the famous poet. But then he opened his mouth, his golden voice transformed the room, the evening, the world...everyone listened, enchanted by his power over language.*

Now I address this letter to Parnassus. May this letter find you, Dylan, in good spirits, and not a coin in your pocket, entirely happy.

Yours affectionately,
Penny

Life's last gift – Jane Spray

Show me your wonders, though there's none to keep.
For memory tricks us, as does time, - try as we might.
Comes, last of all, the sublime gift of sleep.

Though the watch be long, there is a silence, deep
Beyond the stars; the Milky Way glows bright.
Show me your wonders, though there's none to keep.

And sure, for lovers, whose hearts still bound and leap,
Forgetting all, one body through the night,
Comes, last of all, the sublime gift of sleep.

My wide-eyed child, the learning curve is steep -
Young birds, launched from the nest, take tumbling flight.
Show me your wonders, though there's none to keep.

Even for those who lie awake and weep,
Who tussle in the dark, sort wrong from right,
Comes, last of all, the sublime gift of sleep.

Spent bodies all, that to the bed's foot creep,
No need for rage, if this is kept in sight:
Show me your wonders, though there's none to keep.
Come, last of all, the sublime gift of sleep.

Inspired by *'Do not go gentle into that good night'*

Dear Dylan

I was very sorry to hear of the death of your father. A kind, brave, God-cursing man. I love your poems, their music, energy and wild imagery. The lyric life that is in them. Do not go gentle, and Elegy are fine ones to remember your father by.

When Martin and I had a baby, Martin took a year off work, unpaid, and the three of us went travelling. One place we stayed was a damp cottage in Blaenau Ffestiniog, cut into and against the steep, slate hillside. When it rained, and it rained a lot, all the fall from the hill bubbled up and flowed through the cottage, eventually seeping out the front; slowly drying out when the weak sun shined and streaked once more.

When our friend came back from her Mediterranean holiday, she rummaged in the attic, and brought down a huge, brown teddy bear, as a gift for Rowan. This bear is over a yard tall, sitting down!

We named the bear Dylan, in your honour. He is fond of reciting your poems, in a sonorous, sometimes sozzled, lilt.

Long may your 'heart's truth still be sung', by yourself, and our favourite bear.

Thank you.
Jane

Hireath, three ways – Hannah Stone

When my brow was un-furrowed
and my heart still rose each morning
singing out its hopes, I left the metropolis,
headed north with the prince of my life,
lugging dreams as worthless as a new penny
but twice as bright. What were these dales
but green swathes of pasture,
with curly-horned sheep scatted like confetti
between walls of stone hewn from a hard land
of flat vowels and few smiles?
Now I crave my Wharfedale walks,
squeeze in the lark's call and damask clouds
between the rumble of wheeled cases
carrying tourists' to-dos, for I also belong
to the bold squares spied on
by tall sash windows of Georgian houses.
And when I beat the bounds of Bloomsbury,
my nose twitches for its fix
of seaweed and saltspray, feet itch for
the cliffs of Pembrokeshire I call my own,
though I share it with a surfeit of seals
and, oh, so many gulls and crows.
So when I settle beside a pile of books,
a glass of something and a blank page
I rest myself, in poetry. But something niggles,
like the pea beneath the twenty mattresses.
The princess never truly feels at home.

Dear Dylan

Even addressing you sounds out the lilt and swagger of your life; the vowels proximate but distinct, the firm rock of the repeated 'd' a buffer against the liquid vowels.

I have in front of me one of your worksheets. Neat towers of lines of rhymes, some underlined and ticked; dent, dint, dinner. I'm glad this archived work-in-progress didn't topple into the 'beer and butter' of your student rooms where poem drafts rustled like the crust of autumn leaves in Milk Wood, where, tonight and every moonless night, lover moan and mourn for their dead dreamers.

Some say you sold out, letting the Third Programme broadcast *Under Milk Wood* to London cognoscenti, with no transmission bending the airwaves to the watery world of the Taf estuary.

But that was you, a Janus poet, one side leaning to the Welsh and one to the wildness across the border, like Mrs Cherry Owen's two husbands, one drunk and one sober, and don't we love them both?

Maybe if I could down several whiskeys in a row I could write like you.

Thanks, anyway.
Hannah

The Writing Shed – Simon Tonkin

We passed each other in the hall, my brain pristine, uninjured then
While you were adding an insult to yours. 1953
A black and white, Rollie McKenna type, world away; a decade yet
From the flashbulb memory of J.F.K. Now I'm old enough to smell death,
I'm visiting the shed where you professed time would no longer let you play
And be without his means to mercy, Where the gossip fresh Taf
Meets the salt, sullen sea, around the tide drawn continents
Of your burnished estuary, where you looked out across
This just kissed, glistening mouth and listened to the stalking curlews,
The sad contentment of their cry, lamenting when a page outstared you.
In the curious trees, straining their necks to see the Boathouse
Blue-black hearted jackdaws, sentinels for the castle ruins,
Fix me with their half-cocked stare, pin me with their mean sneers.
Wood pigeons tease in playground metre and all the gulls
Are raucous as drunks. At this hour, going this way,
Along the stone cold sober lane, your long idle shed of the stale,
The impatient, the stubborn line; your `water and tree room'
Locked against Time. How often did you ignore its peeling door,
Unable to face the bare altar of a page and so Cliff Walk your way
To the nearest glass of Buckley's Best and a guilty game of Nap?

How my heart rambles by your graveside, you are part of St. Martin's now.
The shadow of the whitest cross in the monumental copse of the churchyard,
Cat at rest on your bones. Just over the hill, I know, the estuary
Is emptying again, the mud shoals with their crushed spines of sand
Are becoming exposed. Overhead, another quicksilver sliver of a jet
Is slicing open the flesh of the singing, gathering blue, going west,
Dead set on America. Its trace is streaming back so easy and teeming
From its inner spinning place, only to slowly dissipate
In the once young heaven of its wake.

Dear Ditch,

I'm the opposite of you; I'm only a poet when I'm not writing. But just like you, it was the only thing I thought to do – from the very start – just the one idea.

I've no glorious token of identity – as Cat would have described it. You thought the world was half the devil's and half your own. I thought that too, once upon a time. No more. Now I know it all belongs to others.

I imitated your poetry in the hope that by rubbing up against a great poet I could pass myself off as one. But your tragedy was to do with your wonderful unadulterated childhood – while with me it was the enchanted carnival of my youth.

If we share anything in common it is that we were both crippled by nostalgia. Nostalgia is the curse of the lost. But I've never set anyone's heart ablaze with words I've gathered myself and you have.

What did you write to a fan once... *Don't let my stuff stop you writing?*

You must have been so confident it would do exactly that... it certainly did for me in the end.

Yours
Simon

Portrait of the Artist Among Underdogs – Deborah Tyler-Bennett

No matter how comely, poems tread paths between
this world and our next, serenading those neglected.

Welsh Dylan knew it. Clocked that hunchback
in the park, his tethered self. Followed close
lone morning songs and nocturnes.

Come back, Seraphic Boyo!
All breakfast, noon and night, cry my Market
Town's deep undertow: Girl spooking a closed
shop's entry, crowds eyed for change, stretched
arms, sinewy larches; doorway occupant – throaty
in weasel dark, mongrel a mobile sheepskin.

Wind with them through scarlet apple stalls,
fish-heads gawping, mustard-crusty hams
to nightshade parks, where such become
shadows, shivering 'till cock-crow.

Amen their hopes, come back, Seraphic Boyo,
read loves, dreams, rest, via the poem's braille,
lines tracing whorled stones. Sudden art, the
filigree of park gates, bricks smooth as fire-
glazed toffee apples prized by truant boys.

Inspired by *'The Hunchback in the Park'*

Dear Dylan,

Just to say, you were right on all-things poetry ... and prose ... Writing for voices, radio in your head, passion play spilling-out to eager listeners.

Because of you, I've imagined such listeners every time I've written. Your Wales, my Nottinghamshire, I think you'd love the people I grew with. Daily, try setting them down to do you justice, fail, partly succeed, living to try. You'd've made much of Great Aunt Lucy, following the road mender's cart – dustpan and brush primed: "mind out me way, you mucky so-and-so."

Or Mrs Oak, breasting fences prow-like, saying of someone power walking (long before the term existed): "Good day to you, Sir, walking I see." When he'd gone from sight adding: "Just look at that! Silly old sod learned nowt."

Pub chatter, beery talk, sniping in Butchers' queues – you'd catch them. I think of your hunchback in the park, ask who treads his dark path now? Lovers, chancers, fighters, charlatans – just try and catch their cadences.

Radio in my head tuned to your channel. Technology changes. But, Oh Dylan, thanks to you, the frequency remains the same. So, as Celts have it, 'set the stars ablaze'.

Yours in wonder ....
Deborah

Skomer – Steve Walter

And the guttering red rock
sliced like decks of cards
slanted into the sea.

And she is there in the mist
in the sea breeze she
is in the gathering dark
she rides the mounting forces
which rise beneath the blackening waves
and she is in the quilted sky

she is there in the billowing
sheeted veils of the afternoon
and in the rakish cry of the gulls
screaming over the graves of shearwater
skeletons, she is at the exits of hollowed burrows
among bits of dead bird, dead rabbit, scattered
beside the remains of Iron Age homesteads
and she is marking the way
in Celtic stone against the unforgiving grey.

Inspired by: *'In my Craft or Sullen Art'*

Dear Dylan

I had hoped to meet you, but by the time I got to the dock, your boat had left for New York. Your voice, always full of the music of the wild land and the sea. I stood there beside you, in your boathouse at Laugharne, but you could not see me. The open sea, gently slap, slapping, the timbers below.

My father loved you too, as he loved Wales, and our holidays were with you. We shared a love of life, of community, in the silence of your craft. My Dad wrote poetry. We listened to Sibelius.

And yet, you died at less than two-thirds of my age. Of course, I would've shared a pint or two, perhaps a whiskey chaser, but then again we would have stopped short of cutting your years, and killing your verse, somehow would have healed that bronchitis. Mates for a moment, rooting around for the source of words.

Dad embraced the spirit of the dragon, and told us stories of Brown Bear, Robot and Sad Dragon.

And there were the elements of your laughter, that gave us joy, and by contrast the sullen roots of life.

Yours,
Steve

Body of the Former Maria – Jennifer Wilson

The sea in its coagulopathy leaves you here
to lie upon the rocks, reducing
the fluids of your body to their salts
and separate waters.

Birds cry as they break your skin & swell,
sucking up the sodium of your bed.

How uncomfortably we lie here –
prevailing westerlies washing our flesh
to bone and wasting
our hair to weeds.

Deaf with a thousand waves
beneath you, I keep you,
shelter your head from harm.
I clear your raw skin red,
clean your lungs to make a breath.

I will watch over you,
sea-shaped and shaken
of my edge.

I will let the sand
soften me.
I will take you
from this death.

Dear Dylan,

It was water on the lungs, of course, that came to claim you. I hear it, vast as your voice, full of God come apart as He made it so unbeautiful and imperfect as I look into my child's eyes – Grey blue, steely, wet.

I have kissed the salt from his skin on the quayside, watched the seabirds dive. I think of you in the water. I think of the water taking you. My own imperfect words were never so lovely.

O forgive me. I think of you when I think of birth.

Jennifer

At Afon Gwili – Jacquie Wyatt

There was an oak tree on the hill opposite
thistles that stung purple when grasped,
piles of eweberries to be avoided
clover flowers, exploding dandelions
spores drifting through days as
this small ghost of me spiralled out
of control around emptied bottles. Picking
dandelions made you wet the bed.

Dylan's ghost walked alongside me down
Afon Gwili, made weed-bed rugs yield under
my feet, pushed off sharp pebbles flexing
in the water's relentless snatch.
He whispered that Welsh rivers
are parasites that strangle growth
fix flailing limbs to memories like stones
they will only let you escape through
a lyrical phrase, a poisonous yearning

to be young again, cartwheeling
without consequence, to be all
entrances. The conduit tongue
of a god before it got stilled
by self-contempt; before death
stamped *was* on his brow. Was
a Welsh poet, a playwright, a lover,
Swansea's most famous boozy son.
Reputation louder now than words,
runs as wild as weeds.

Inspired by *On Fern Hill, Death and Entrances* & *Poem on his Birthday*

Dear Dylan,

I hate you. I appreciate you're dead but even alive you'd have no interest in why. I'm told I'm banal, sickly, mental. I lie heavy around certain people's necks, all bagged-up longing. I am a waste of breath.

Pure beast, unlike you. *I hold a beast, an angel, and a madman in me.* My son is all three too. His eyes twitch as if that beeping machine gives tiny electric shocks. I hope that, in his dreams, he outruns his soiled self.

Modelled on you. Do you find that funny? Funnier still, I modelled myself on your Caitlin: *Dylan had this rather odd view that all the best poets died young.*

Of course we lived wildly. Whatever Caitlin and I stored got snatched away. You said: *though lovers be lost, love shall not.* That is a lie. Most lovers are lost because they've stopped loving. One learns to stop loving a vacuum.

My boy says it's cheap vodka makes him sick. If I'd give him cash he could drink better wines. Face the colour of urine, he calls me selfish.

His poetry-loving father named him Dylan after you. My boy won't make forty either.

Jacquie

Indigo Dreams Publishing
24 Forest Houses
Halwill
Beaworthy
Devon
EX21 5UU
www.indigodreams.co.uk